*All children have
a strong desire to read
to themselves...*

*and a sense of achievement when they can do so.
The* **read it yourself** *series has been devised to
satisfy their desire, and to give them that sense
of achievement. The series is graded for specific
reading ages, using simple vocabulary and
sentence structure, and the illustrations
complement the text so that the words and
pictures together form an integrated whole.*

LADYBIRD BOOKS, INC.
Lewiston, Maine 04240 U.S.A.
© LADYBIRD BOOKS LTD MCMLXXVII
Loughborough, Leicestershire, England

Printed in England

Red Riding Hood

by Fran Hunia
illustrated by Kathie Layfield

Ladybird Books

This is Red Riding Hood.

She is at home
playing with her toys.

Red Riding Hood's mother
says, "Come here,
Red Riding Hood.
Grandma is at home in bed.
I have some cakes for her.
I want you to go
and give the cakes
to Grandma, please."

"Yes," says Red Riding Hood.
"I want to go
and see Grandma.
I will give her the cakes."

Mother gives the cakes
to Red Riding Hood.

"Good-by,"
says Red Riding Hood.

"Good-by,"
says her mother.
"See that the big bad wolf
does not get you."

Red Riding Hood sees
some flowers
in the woods.

"Grandma likes flowers,"
she says.
"I will pick some flowers
for Grandma."

The big bad wolf
sees Red Riding Hood.

"Come and play with me,"
he says.

"No," says Red Riding Hood.
"I cannot play with you.
I have to go
and see Grandma.
She is in bed.
I have some cakes
and flowers for her."

The wolf runs
to Grandma's house.

He says, "Grandma, Grandma,
I want to come in."

Grandma is in bed.

"Is that you,
Red Riding Hood?"
she asks.

"Yes," says the big bad wolf.

Grandma gets up.

She sees the wolf.

"Help, help," she says.

She climbs up
into a cupboard.

The big bad wolf comes in.

He gets Grandma's cap
and shawl, and jumps
into Grandma's bed.

Red Riding Hood
has the cakes
and the flowers.

She comes
to Grandma's house.

"Grandma," she says,
"it is Red Riding Hood.
Can I come in, please?"

"Yes," says the big bad wolf.
"You can come in.
I want to see you,
Red Riding Hood."

Red Riding Hood comes in.
She says, "Look, Grandma.
I have some cakes
and some flowers for you."

She looks at the wolf.

He is in Grandma's bed.

He has Grandma's cap
and shawl on.

"You have big eyes,
Grandma,"
says Red Riding Hood.

"Yes," says the wolf.
"They are good
to see you with."

"You have big ears,
Grandma,"
says Red Riding Hood.

"Yes," says the wolf.
"They are good
to hear you with."

"You have big teeth,
Grandma,"
says Red Riding Hood.

"Yes," says the big bad wolf.
"They are good
to eat you with."

The wolf jumps up.

''Help, help,''
says Red Riding Hood.

She runs out of the house.

Red Riding Hood sees
a man.

It is her father.

"Help, help," she says.
"Here comes a wolf.
He is a big wolf.
He wants to eat me up."

"Get up into a tree,
Red Riding Hood,"
says her father.

"I can get
that big bad wolf."

Red Riding Hood climbs
up into a tree.

Her father gets the wolf.

Red Riding Hood
comes down.

She says, "Please come
and help me
look for Grandma."

They go to Grandma's house.

Grandma is in the cupboard.

"Help, help," she says.
"I want to get down."

Red Riding Hood
and her father
get Grandma down.

They help her into bed.

"I have some cakes
and flowers for you,"
says Red Riding Hood.

She gives the cakes
and flowers to Grandma.

"You are a good girl,"
says Grandma.
"The cakes look good.
We can all have some."

"You eat the cakes, Grandma,"
says Red Riding Hood.
"We have to go home
for supper now.
Come on, Father."

"It was good to see you,"
says Grandma.
"Here is an apple for you
and one for Father.
Good-by, Red Riding Hood."
"Good-by."